Bully Pulpit

By

Kim Bridgford

ISBN-13:978-0615694153

Author photo by Marion Ettlinger

Cover photo and design by Pete Duval

White Violet Press
1840 West 220th Street, Suite 300
Torrance, California 90501

For Nick and Pete

For all those who have ever been bullied

Table of Contents

"the way we hover over the past, bring it to life, or find, to our surprise, that it has a life of its own, turning and turning and turning in space"

Brigit Pegeen Kelly, "The Sparrow's Gate,"
The Orchard

***

"If G--- were a man, it would be different, but we don't live in those times."

Anonymous I, 2009

"Go forth and set the world on fire."

St. Ignatius of Loyola

I.

Public

"Tyler was a fine young man, and a distinguished musician. The family is heartbroken beyond words."

Statement from Tyler Clementi's family

"Anyone with iChat, I dare you to video chat me between the hours of 9:30 and 12:00."

Dharun Ravi, Tyler's roommate

Before Jumping Off the Bridge

For Tyler Clementi, cyber bullied to his death

"Jumping off the gw bridge sorry."
Tyler's suicide note

I loved to play the violin, to hear
The notes before I felt them in my hands,
That process: a god of sunlight with all ends
Before beginnings, unbitten apple, air

Unsnaked and pure. When privacy was gone—
My life-in-life—it scoured out my soul.
I knew it wouldn't end, this kiss and tell
I didn't tell. Those arrows can't be seen,

Must be felt, the kind of drawn-out note
That rests inside the wellspring of your throat.
I don't pretend to understand what loves
The meanness that results in ruined lives.

It's the music I jump into, and the mouthing
Of love. You know, how a kiss dissolves to nothing.

Mobbing

"*Mobbing. . . '*...an emotional assault.
It begins when an individual becomes the target
of disrespectful and harmful behavior. Through
innuendo, rumors, and public discrediting, a
hostile environment is created in which one
individual gathers others to willingly, or
unwillingly, participate in continuous
malevolent actions.'"

*Mobbing: An Emotional Assault in the American
Workplace*

For Phoebe Prince

Birds do it, and so do girls. They gather,
And show the target that she doesn't matter,
That she's an "Irish whore," or she's a bitch.
There are ways to make a target need a crutch.

Adults do it. They find someone exceptional,
Spread rumors, say that she is trouble, a "complainer,"
Make her do others' work. Then she's a whiner.
There are no rules, and nothing's rational.

Even hanging was preferable to life.
So people rewrote history in their grief.

Birds gather, and they peck, and they attack,
To stay within the safety of the flock.

Relentless, the mindlessness of beaks.
It's just like that with people. No one speaks.

Flowers

For the victims of bullycide

This sonnet is for Debbie Shaw, Michaela
Kendall, Roger Hillyard and for Kelly Yeomans.
This sonnet is for those who felt the demons
Of others' rage: for Darren Steel, Melissa
Chamblis. And it's for those who reach for pills,
For guns, for help, for sympathy, for rope.
This poem's for Stephen Windhall, and for hope.

And where are all the names of those who took
The vulnerable and weak and made a hook?
Some call these troubled children, either side.
But it's the victims—hopeless—who have died.

Somewhere the fragrance of compassion spills.

This sonnet will give voice to Brian Head.
And Jared Benjamin High is also dead.

Song in the Canoe

Uneven, all the early worlds will go,
The way a shiver runs down all the snow,
And dies. There is a thing in people meant
To make them flawed and different.

And everybody dies, and if one body sings,
It puts change inside the kingdom. Take one man,
Who sang his heart out in an old canoe
Because he was commanded, and a Jew.

Within the framework of reality
There is a shift inside the ordinary.
Afterwards, like a tablecloth on things,
There is a smoothing out of what went on.

For instance, people listening to the song,
They thought it was so beautiful, this wrong.

Blood Doesn't Have Your Name

For Ryan White

Blood is blood. It doesn't have your name,
Your personality, your goals, your favorite
Color and all the things that make triumphant
The individual experience you frame.

How people like to give a lasting taste
To something, label unknown things a crime.
It's what the *mean* in us does all the time.
The disease was new, and you were just its host.

Courage has a name. It gets up every day.
It wears a sadness that others will not touch.
It learns it's best not to expect too much.
It learns that bullies rule and fear the day.

Words: *AIDS, hero, hemophiliac.*
Once words are said, you cannot take them back.

Sit

For Rosa Parks

Sit down. Take years of tired off your feet.
Take others' problems, and give them a voice.
Try not to think of hoses, dogs, and hate,
Or what will happen when you make a choice.

Sit down. It feels so good. The dignity,
The claim you've made to innate humanness.
And once you do it, it becomes so easy:
To be in love with almost-permanence.

When I sit down, I think of you, the ride
Through history that you would then engage.
Determination rides on tears of rage
And makes them tears of reconciliation.
They are the kind of tears that heal the nation.
It's in the transformation history's made.

Somewhere

"I've learned that people will forget what you said, people will forget what you did, but people will never forget how you made them feel."

Maya Angelou

Somewhere in the dark you'll hear the crying,
For, in the end, it's "how someone makes you feel."
Somewhere, by his own hand, a teen is dying

From bullying, by being pushed, by trying,
Against all odds, to be an individual.
Somewhere in the dark you'll hear the crying.

It changes everything: public displaying
Of someone else's shame. Now vulnerable,
Somewhere, by her own hand, a teen is dying.

The bullies always say they were just playing,
Or making group dynamics manageable.
Somewhere in the dark you'll hear the crying.

And it is not a game: to be there, sighing
On the cross; to be the target on the wall.
Somewhere, by his own hand, a teen is dying.

The world, like this, can't last. In the end, I'm saying
It's joy that is the answer to the soul.
Somewhere in the dark you'll hear the crying.
Somewhere, by her own hand, a teen is dying.

II

Private

"I personally guarantee you will never hold another leadership position again."

Explanation: "Everything you touch turns to gold."

Anonymous I, 2009

"Have you seen *Rashomon*?. . . Everybody has a side."

Anonymous II, response to academic workplace
bullying, 2009

***

"Love and hope and faith are the virtues of the impossible, taking the measure of the immeasurable future. The borders of the possible are safe but flat, sure but narrow, well defined but confining, and they stake out the lines of an unsalted and mediocre life, without a passionate hope, where nothing *really* happens and all present systems will do just fine. If at the end of our lives we find that all our hopes have been sensible and moderate and measured by the horizon of the future present, if we have never been astir with the impossible, then we shall also find that on the whole life has passed us by....The religious sense of life has to do with exposing oneself to the radical uncertainty and the open-endedness of life."

John D. Caputo, *On Religion*

Genealogy

after "The Blue Terrance,"
by Terrance Hayes

I come from people who laughed and said they were birthed
from pirates who threw the "e" from "Bridgeford" into the ocean,
onto the back and forth trundle of the rough, salt air,
because, in the New World, you can start out fresh,
be economical; on the other side of the family,
children were taken away—Helen, whose legs never grew,
like a human fish swimming through the bottoms of chairs,
the other who was nameless, deaf. They died in a mental hospital.
Those things happen, my grandmother said,
as if she had just fried up liver and onions and eaten them clean.
Her stepfather once chased her around the table, and slapped her
when she read the newspaper—not for reading it
and learning something, but for not knowing how to make it
look unread. I come from people who know how to work,
who work as if life itself were work—and it is,
joy an iris almost translucent, done in a shade of purple
too delicate to describe. Marriage, death, pain—these are to be
    endured—
but let a child be named or food be prepared, and everybody has
an opinion. Casseroles appear, held in hands roughened
from bleach, rings too tight and attached to flesh
pulling weeds from the ground with such force
dirt skitters off and cowers in the grass.
I come from women who have given up everything for their men
but their children, their love like a handmade scarf too
    embarrassing
for the outside world. I come from men who late in life
discovered their jobs had abandoned them, the gold watches
and plaques inadequate for the hours spent away from home.
I come from a place where dreams were clumsy on the big, wide
    lines

of elementary school, then wadded up because you had
to take care of others who had given up for you, who had had lives
given up for *them*, and this giving up was a contract
you signed before you were born. You did not move away
to cities like New York, dirty, full of strangers,
because belief in our Lord Jesus Christ was like a name tag to be
    read
by thieves. On the Fourth of July, my grandfather,
in his madness, took my son too close to a bonfire, pointing
out the flickering landscape, and all I could do
was run toward them. I always thought my story was about
my grandmother, who loved my mother because she was
her precious thing, along with my sister,
and throughout my youth I navigated my grandmother's will,
pitiless and ready to cut, burn, clean, or drink
in the same mood. When I was six she fed me salt
instead of sugar because she could, April Fooled me
into thinking she had bought me a kitten. She was a survivor, too.
I come from a drive-through town, where you could go to church,
or die as a teenager on the winding, unlit roads,
and where, one day, I opened a book,
the way people understand they are adopted,
crisp and clean and unapologetic as a raindrop
sitting on a leaf. I am like a foreign tongue
come home to roost, taking up the old language,
its polysyllabic mysteries and complicated syntax
revived with the attention of the beloved engaging in a music
so perfect it breaks. I come home to rest,
to be who I was, whoever that was, driving through the shadows
of the cut-down trees, circling the new trees naked as gifts
that no one wants. But they, too, grow: they grow up.

Ruined People

Is it just Eden we're talking about, ducking guiltily
Out of the dark wood, the sodden mysteries—
What we could have been and what we can still be,
But aren't? Shame settles like a fierce whiff
Of stench along the rib cage. The gate is iron; the bars are cold.
The angels, unfathomable as a lost language,
As elaborate as hieroglyphs, stand with their feathers stiff,
White, and unextended, like a promise
No one can be forced to bear. What I am saying is,
Is it *in* us? Not a place? The moment between the way we shine
And the way we don't? Even a woman on a cell phone
Pushing an elderly woman out of the way
In a supermarket, or a harsh epithet
Yelled out of callousness or hurt,
About race, or age, or gender, or sexual orientation,
Makes me want to weep. Why do we give up?
Why are we silent? Once my cousin told me
About how she had been asked, at seven,
To clean the grout in the bathroom with a toothbrush,
Those fierce long lines leading everywhere—
And later was slapped for touching drapes, for doing this,
For *not* doing that, and couldn't
Have a birthday party, although her sister could,
Not the Barbie birthday cake, Barbie's sweet white frosting dress,
And those perfect lips, thin as a rosebud curl,
Not even the balloons:
And these things surface like hot sticky insects
Out of a marsh gone putrid with rage,
Years later. The drinks pile up.
It matters who makes the decisions. It matters
Who is in control. The quiet in the dark,
And a teen watches her screen light up

In the scent of her own lip gloss, her delight
At her age and the candle-lit belief in human goodness, which
Is Eden after all, the wind blowing its age-old touch
Of forgiveness through the fruit-bearing trees; then words
Take her spirit and fling it down, the way a dog does
A rabbit, something quick and mean and unawares,
A velvet rag gone still. By morning
She is dead; she's out of it now.
She couldn't stand what they'd been saying, until she couldn't
Stand herself. I've been there too, been bullied like that,
And it's both intimate and general, like someone's
Kicked you in the teeth, and forgotten who
You are. If Eden is in us, then so is hell. And this was at work.
I saw a movie where a man convinced himself he loved a woman, believed
In his own myth to such a point that when she told him,
Just before she died, that he made her sick, that she
Had only done what she had to do to survive,
He pissed on her. What he had loved
Was hating her, as finely tuned as a wine
That people wait decades to savor in the back
Of their mouths. But her crime
Was saying what was true. *So there.* The last dollop
Of pee as if she was just the dirt
Itself. You can think that what you do alone
In the dark, you can think that what you do
Doesn't have consequences, but someone
Is always watching. And those angels,
What do they say?, hanging out at the garden,
Their white soft texture like creased vintage capes
Far-flung with pearls, and flickering, flickering
In and out of the trees. What do they say to

26

Kicked? Clubbed? Attacked by dogs?
Water boarded? That these people are ruined?
That their lives are ruined?
When I was younger, and pulled a thread,
That's the term they used, "ruined."
That's how you did it to a sweater,
And sometimes you couldn't help yourself.
You would pull until it made you want
To see the puckering, to see the fine clean line
Made into something you destroyed. Don't pull, you were told;
Leave it alone. At a certain point, things could still be fixed;
You could show restraint, could nurse it almost whole.
Yet if you knew you had reached a limit to yourself
And couldn't do good, couldn't face your own sorry self,
You did that—*pulled*—so that if you couldn't be God in the world,
You could at least be other than yourself, you could
Escape into this lost and ruined thing. Destroy it even.
People suffer, they go on. That's our nature,
Even with the gate swung shut. Yesterday,
Inside a market, a man yelled at me,
And I turned in a crowd of strangers,
To hear him say, "You dropped your glove."
It seemed like a rose on a stage, dramatic as a bird,
Sprawled and woolen. I kneeled
To pick it up. When I gestured "Thank you,"
You would think the heavens had opened.
Eden. No wonder they left. It's so hard. Looking
Back at all that blissful shining, the long last lick of innocence,
    who can
Stand it? Yet who can stand anything
Without it?

Commandments

Maybe it all gets back to the word "commandments,"
People fancying themselves Moses, or God,
The beard confused with a cloud, and the words
As searing as language fired
Into a tablet. When the dust is blown off,
There is language, and the law.
Until I went through this—
People who would do anything
For their word to be law—
I thought the commandments
Were shining. "I personally guarantee
You will never hold another leadership position again,"
And my heart slammed shut.
"You didn't have drinks with the right people," he said.
"We don't want you." When I complained,
I was told, "Everybody has a side."
When my pastor's son broke his leg,
He had to wear a partial body cast
Because of his muscular dystrophy.
In the movies there's a miraculous cure,
But in life you sing with your father,
Holding a candle, and your all-out belief
Breaks the heart of everyone in the audience.
I don't know. Commandments.
I have trouble with words that can bludgeon you;
I have trouble with kneeling down:
Not to God, but to people who make life
Into a private show of their own inadequacies,
Swimming in late-night drinks, and everybody
Has to live with this: the late-night petty e-mails,
The preference for women to be meek.
I'm a true believer, I guess. I still see the apples

Shining on the trees, their golden skins tawny
As everything I've ever wanted to happen,
The angels rustling in the background,
Their wings like the possibility
I see in my son's shoulder blades,
Erupting into astonishment.
The angels in the garden: they want it to work out,
Like leaves curving their gestures
Into vivid green, the flowers rimmed with scent.
Of course, there will be snakes around fruit.
In my old life, at my old house,
The man mowing our lawn told us
That someone's pet snake was hanging
From one of our apple trees, and his fear
Was like sweat. He had to stop. He was already
Fashioning the story into one of the myths
Of his life, how the snake looked at him from the leaves,
How he had to make a decision. When we walked out
To take a look, to see this hidden thing in the orchard,
It had already slithered away.
Of course, it was not Satan. You could see how they could be
Confused; you could see how someone
Would want to command. Perhaps it's just like
This snake ending up in a tree, bored
And amoral, munching on apples. I don't know.
Stepping out of the structure of my life
Was like stepping into the wind;
It was like jumping off a high ridge into the future.
Until then, I never saw everyone's failings,
But when you lose your wonder, you see how everyone
Is ruined. This is how people grow old, I think,
Seeing how small everyone is, how little

They are willing to do, how in the end
They do nothing. And this was nothing
Compared to all that people go through in their lives:
Illness, poverty, racism, war.
My grandmother would sit and cry
Sometimes when we opened our Christmas gifts—
The largesse of all the piles made her happy
(Her family: who could believe it?), and also made her sick—
Because she remembered the days of opening nothing,
The church baskets that meant
She was charity, that meant she had to
Make choices to survive. You have to get your wonder back
Or die. I had to find a new dream,
Forgiveness like an answer hanging on every leaf.
I can't go along to get along—that's not how
I was raised—it has to be right:
It has to be an excellence
So astonishing the mere thought of it
Takes your breath away. That's the only way
I can live. Not these scolding commandments,
Not these arbitrary rules. Who can live this
Empty life? Who can live with the guilt?
When the tablets are broken, what do you do?
Disappear or shine?

Unfairness

How you wake up and the world tastes like mud, and still
You have to go on, with everyone watching,
And you're the one with the mistake; you're the one
Who has to face the impossible odds. You were born
Knowing you were to die at age twenty, and what's the point
Really: to doing homework, to being there every day, to being
Responsible? My best friend's father, black in the days
When being black meant trusting the fragile thread
Extended by white people, worked all day for cash money
And was given bags of old clothes and rotten food,
And what was he to do? To complain was to say
You were better than the system.
The police came with their sirens and their eyes
In sunglasses rimmed with one truth:
That what you said did not matter.
By better, I mean unfairness sits in the mouth
Of excellence; unfairness turns dreams to dust,
And it's coming out of that, not dwelling
On the ordinary malice of broken human beings
And using your time for excellence, transforming
This pain into hope that is so hard. Because you think,
During everybody's suffering,
Why are you doing this? To what end?
When it could be so astonishing?
And so how did you do it, Rosa,
Day after day, sitting at the back of the bus,
Doing what you have to because it's life, after all,
Then one day not rise, not give up your seat?
There are people who need to make others feel small
To feel who they are, to feel important,
And what do you get in the end but "making people
Do things"? And then what? "Most people when you

Shut them down stay shut down, but you keep coming back":
What does it mean to be a person who says such a thing,
What has happened to morality,
When did it soften to mud, to snakes, to sorrow?
What happened to you, I wonder?
Was it your son who did that to you,
The unfairness of what had happened to him?
Was it other people's pain, like a drink
Far into the bottle, that felt better than love?
Even though people had lost all respect for you,
You didn't care. At least, you thought,
You could make them obey.

Evil

Is a feeling, swinging on the hour,
Its thick intention hanging like a tire.
Smash, wreck, hurt, undulate, destroy.
For evil holds within itself a joy

Of taking goodness by the hand, so pure
You wouldn't know the difference from a flower,
Like love, it is a hot and sudden arrow.
Like shame, it layers time with fig-leaf sorrow,

And pulls the curtain wing-spread off a fly,
With iridescent viciousness, to splay
The intersection between *do* and *don't.*
It's clear the bitter message that's been sent.

Don't underestimate it: that hot note
That whispers in your ear and cuts your throat.

Watching

Someone inside the group is isolated.
You know something is wrong, but you endure it.
You tell yourself the target is not *hated,*

Just being taught a lesson. That's what's needed:
And everyone's worst impulse wants to jeer at
Someone. Inside, the group is insulated.

Inside your dreams are moments where you play it
Differently. You take the hands of merit.
You tell yourself the target is not hated;

Besides, you're happy it's not *you* that's baited.
You do not speak because you know you fear it,
As someone inside the group (and not deleted).

You think there will be a time when evil's sated,
When normalcy is back, and you can share it.
You tell yourself the target is not hated.

Then everything goes wrong, as if it's fated.
In time, it's like hot water. You can bear it.
Someone inside the group is isolated.
If you don't speak, the cycle is repeated.

Brokenness

Men like a little brokenness in women.
That's why they put them on a pedestal:
To knock them down, and make them feel more human.

A stumble? Not a problem. "Might have been"
Is better than to have nothing at all.
Men like a little brokenness in women.

Do not invite them to be keynote then;
Some adjunct work will fill the time meanwhile.
The hard-knock life will make them seem more human.

Give them all the advising roles. It's men
Who need the extra time to make a book deal.
Men like a little brokenness in women.

If women win awards, men are forgotten.
There are ways to keep the women from the table.
When they knock on your door, just be inhuman.

It's better, then, to shut achievement down.
Discrimination usually is subtle.
Men like a little brokenness in women.
Knock. Them. Down. But you are only human.

Licked

Unfairness licks your face
With its bitter and hungry tongue
And you cry, "Foul." You cry, "Faith."
Otherwise, for the praising part,
You think you can get along without it:
Your eyes cat-happy with the cream
Of your life, the purr of circumstance
Massaging your contours. Take a bite
Into mean or nasty, and you let out a howl.

Is this what they've been talking about?
This taste?

Like a bridle pulled against your teeth.

Yet, maybe, when there's something to praise,
The sensual curvature of your success,
You won't think it's your due,
Won't think it's all you.

Paradise

You put your head up past the world, red dress
Dropping its petals back. And now the top,
Followed by a zip code sky address.
You just have to be willing to look up.

Good-bye illuminated, lost late skin,
To tell you all the past you've walked out in.
Welcome the ferrying texture of the fern,
The tight embroidery, and then the turn

Where soul steps barefoot out onto the air,
(No corrugated strap: just open stair).
Each step a footprint rubbing out the price
Of rotten pennies, leaves, and sacrifice,

You never thought it was so easy, this
Kiss before you knew it was a kiss.

What Happened

I came out the other side,
The way the weather tries on another kind of cool
And shifts the wind in places. Who was this girl
Who stood in a brown cotton dress and a row of bangs,
One hand on a metal railing, and assessed
The pine trees' sprawling certitude, their flavors sucking on sap?
I had left her behind, distance in her eyes, the yelp
Of a difficult lane and darkness like a drug.
I floated on the edge of pain, edge of self,
The mask of perfection clinging to my skin
Like a message to a bottle, scalloping the waves.
I liked that woman with her paper doll life,
Cut with gold stars.

Later, hurt and heaved to the air, I wondered where God was,
The way I had as a girl, pleated, eyes on the future.
At night, on the lane, I was so afraid—
All the spooks lived there with their brambly fingers—
The gnats dancing on thorns of fruit
And in the *swish-swish* of the meadow.
The fingers reached out and said things to me
That I didn't want to hear, terrible things,
About what life could do to you, and I felt it
Under my skirt, the way I knew secrets.
The breath, I remember, was both hot and cool,
Like alcohol putting its lips
Around the slim coffin of a cigarette.
Far-off the trucks barreled down the drowsy plenitude of roads,
But on the lane the fire flies winked, and winked again,
And there was no goodness to it, that light,
Just the heart misreading those stunned creatures
Into code, into things you want to put in a jar
And study into sense.

I wanted to say, "This is so wrong." I wanted to say, "Stop,"
But when you are older, evil puts on shabby clothes
And dresses in the style of hypocrisy.
It's the smallness in the end that does you in.
When you are young, bad reaches out from the side of the lane
And grabs you, or cuts the silk out of your life,
But later people say, "You will do what we say or else,"
And if you choose *else,* you don't realize it at first:
Eventually you end up here.

III.

Mythological

"Chaos is come again."

Iago, *Othello*

Part I

The Desdemona Sonnets

Desdemona to Othello

You are a whisperer: of stories made
From bodies stunned from war, where victories choke
On circumstance, and death, and coils of smoke.
Your face is like my journal, just the shade
I like to touch, and worn well into need.

How did this happen? People cannot see
The likeness in a difference, nor will try.
Look! Both of us can kiss, and touch, and bleed.
Ssssh. Listen to the body. It will do.
I'm like the compass heart at home in you.

They tell you it's not you I love, but Cassio.

Don't smother me with anger. Let me go.
My handkerchief, sewn sweet with light and berries,
Is more than gift to me; it is what buries.

Iago to the Audience

At first, I just was curious to see
If I could be the gadfly of the city.
I don't think, then, I named it jealousy,
The two of them so different and so happy.

For that is how it starts, that rancid coil
That snakes its way into you and your soul.
You know you can't make good, and so make evil.
You tell yourself it's just a little trouble.

For that's the way you justify your hate,
And why you never stop to hesitate:
And in the end they'll only call it fate.

A moment hung there, before it was too late.

That he would kill her? Swing her like a cat?
I'm good, but not responsible. For that.

Othello to Desdemona

The strawberries would tell you how I felt—
Your delicacy embroidered there with ease,
Just as I spoke to what you saw in velvet.

What is the language buried in the pause?

That's what we had. A look. A smile. A scratch.
It was unlikely, but it was a match.
When souls unite, it's not exterior.

Iago felt he had to be our courier.

The happiness of others made him see—
Within his eyelids, and within his heart—
That what he had was simply ordinary.
It was our love that hardened him with hurt.

And those who could have stopped it? They are gone.
The guilty are made clean, with blinders on.

Emilia to the Audience

You know how it can be—the *this* and *that*
You trace to what went wrong, the *then* and *now,*
When you feel guilty, responsible somehow.
A handkerchief's a handkerchief, not yet
The motive for the smothering spirit.

If you say I'm at fault, it's hard to hear it.

I love her; she is good. I love him too.
But love does what it does not want to do.

Iago, let me say, does what he pleases.
I know that in a way that's only mine:
Within the dark, he ripples down my spine.

Sometimes, you end up making other choices
Than what you planned for. Love turns into grief,
The world destroyed for one lost handkerchief.

The Pillow to the Handkerchief

We were material, and then, in ways,
Most immaterial, the vehicles
For all the hurt and love of spinning days.
They loved each other, and were miracles.

And though the body is the body, desire
Links the love to love, ignites the liar,
And brings whatever's in them to a blaze.

Othello loved the lightness in her kiss.

As pillow and as handkerchief, we knew
How little and how much we could undo.
For longing as a feeling's under rated,
A gorgeousness that's heat, and silk, and mated
With other longing shivering on a wire,
Beloved to beloved whisperer.

Cassio to Himself

I've always thought the world a shining place
Of truth, and its attendant justice, silver
With an order: not the scaled palaver
That dared to lift the hood of its green face.

Iago never made me pause a minute:
The handkerchief, Iago, Desdemona.
I play them over now, and they still mean the
Same thing. Well, *no*. It's all in how you spin it:

And he could spin the world. Today I'm ruler
Of all the devastation that's been wrought.
It's what I wanted, yet somehow I feel bought.
No, that's not right: now I can be the healer,

And take the chill from off this chilling hour,
The mediocre as our staying power.

Desdemona and Othello Speak from the Afterlife

I'm so glad that you touched me with a scratch;
I'm so glad that you whispered in my ear.
I'm happy that the world was in our reach,
And now this world that makes the farthest near.

We've found the mortal world is not a race;
We've found the normal rules do not apply.
The others are all gone. But in your face—
In your face, I should say—there is the sky.

There is a sadness in the bully's scales.
There is a need that we find we don't have.
There is a lack in him where evil dwells.
I'm sorry that he felt the world should grieve.

Together, with the clouds, we're dark and light:
Irrelevant, who starts as black or white.

Part II

The Persephone Poems

"And the best thing about the legend is
I can enter it anywhere."

Eavan Boland, "The Pomegranate"

Persephone Falls in Love with Hades

She was walking under a curvature of trees
When dizziness overcame her. All she could think of
Was lying down in the shade with him and whispering
While the necklace of diamonds lit up between them
Every time he touched her. So what
That he lived below the earth, below everything;
So what if her life would now be ripped from its spine.
The thrill of what she felt was beyond her,
And even a fingertip of tracing, like a map to a new place,
Made her swoon.

No use telling Mama this. She'd only tell her she was too young,
And being taken advantage of. Who ever came back from such a
    place?
But the earth, now that was something to hang on to.
"Leave me?" her mother asked, out of the prison of bounty.
"Leave this life?" The flowers spun
In their cradles, and gave off whiffs of perfume,
The sky like a wide blue prayer.
No use explaining to anybody.
They warned her, but she felt the lights:
Would know them in the dark.

Later, all the talk was about the pomegranate—
What she ate and didn't eat, why she had to stay.

But the bed?

In the moment, she averted her eyes,
But she knew she would walk there as if on a cord to his voice.

He would hold out his hand. "Baby, baby, baby,"
He might say, then a little bit lower, "Baby, come *on*."
And what was she to do—
Coiled in that hot string, even in her sleep—
What could she do but say *yes*?

Persephone Leads a Double Life

Half the year on earth, half the year below,
She is a woman with a secret smile,
A woman who has found how easy it can be
To step through a door.

Her mother wanted her to stay
In her hometown, join the garden club,
Golf, teach Sunday school at the local church.

What do you do when you have a lover,
And a mother?

You do it all; you walk the line; you move
From six months to six months.
Your dizziness astonishes you.
In the end, of course, your mother
Wanted you to marry someone else.

You do that too.

He is steady, and strong,
And looks at you as if you never live
All those months away.

In the end, you stand on the fault line,
Pray there's no earthquake but your heart.

Persephone Finds Many Aspects of Her Life Have Changed

1.

She can't focus at all,
Or spends all morning thinking
Of the first time Hades touched her,
His hand reaching
With two fingers
For her sex.

Once the polite kiss doubled,
They both knew.

Soon she was reaching everywhere
For stars.

2.

Sometimes she wakes up
To find she's curved around
A thought.

3.

"Come help me clip the roses,"
Says Demeter, and sometimes Persephone cannot
Bear to help. Still, to lose her mother
Would be to lose everything she has ever been:
The girl biting a peach,
The girl writing a story
Everyone knew the ending of.
Demeter pats her hand,

Gives her lockets for Christmas,
Buys styles Persephone hasn't worn
In ten years. "How did you know?"
Persephone says, and Demeter smiles,
Bringing out a coffee cake.

4.

Her mother pretends
That she does not live with Hades
Six months a year. "You're back,
She says, and they go on.
She doesn't want to hear about
The braided story in the dark.
She doesn't want to hear about the spooks, the howls,
The endless feeling of being lost.

5.

Persephone has no more girlfriends;
She turns her cell phone off six months a year,
Escapes to a world she does not
Want to describe to anyone but him.
Just hearing his voice, calling from that other place,
Runs down her like an old-fashioned telephone cord,
Like honey where he touches her.

She'll spend all day parsing a phrase,
Sitting in a daze.

6.

One or the other, one or the other,
And one day Hades says, with a laugh,
Lounging in silk sheets,
"Baby, they call that innocence."

Part III

The Snow White Series

"Imitation is the sincerest form of flattery."

Proverb

The Queen

I was one of those who always said I never
Felt jealousy, for I was so content,
Ruling the world—or mine at least. It went
So wrong. From majesty's long, velvet whir,

I sat apart, and only thought of her:
The repercussions of what people said.
For it wasn't only you, Mirror. Destroyed
By Time, I knew that only one was fair,
And it all rested on the word *compare.*

We didn't need to do that anymore.
Then everything would happen as before.
I'd stand before the crowd as beautiful,
And they'd all answer with their eyes, so full.
I could walk before them, indestructible.

The Mirror

You're old; she's young. It's important that we start
With the plain truth. And then you were foolish in
The way you demonstrated beauty's art:
Or do you remember now that you were vain

In having her kneel, breathless, by the throne,
Her eyes on you? You taught her all she knows,
The apprentice taking, breathless by each rein,
The pleasure of the ride. It's how she rose,

Copycatting all your silken moves,
And when it's done by youth, the grooves
Look more natural than when they are hard won.
In the end, the teacher was too good, the lawn

She walks on smoothed by everything you wear.
It's that, and not her beauty, you can't bear.

The Axe

I yearned to touch that neck; I yearned to cut
The thinnest slice from that most fair of skin,
For, as an instrument, I bear no trace of sin,
But can simply be myself, and then forget

Until I cut again. That is my role:
The way the mirror tells the truth, the way
The apple lifts its poison to the cool
Opening of her lips. The huntsman found her sway

Intoxicating: the look she gave him, bathed
In thanks. He knew he could offer another heart;
He could lie awake at night, his conscience swathed
In all affections that have come apart.

And so I cut the deer. It felt so good,
The fur against my metal, then the blood.

The Poisoned Apple

Inside the basket, I rolled, sweet and dark,
The gift of nature made into a mark.
Some other fruit should take this evil path,
But as things are, I had to suffer with
The queen, for we were two made over. Now
We'd rearrange the world with our knowhow.

Sometimes I tire of snakes, but in the tree
Will rest the diamond thickness, given sway,
To sinew its equation, eyes like slits,
And confabulate the sinner with its glitz.

What a world we live in. I would play my role,
And roll into her hand, to take my toll.
Sometimes, as representative of wrong,
I wish my taste would open up with song.

Sleepy

She made us lose ourselves, as seven men
Gone drowsy with her beauty, with her way
Of loving all of us, yet with the key
To making us each feel that we had won
Her heart. We dreamt of her, and were divided,
But we pretended that our lives were just
The way they'd always been. We found we needed
Her. Ironically, we all were lost.

It's true that we were happier as dwarves,
Without her. It's true, as well, that fortune swerves
And makes a different story, one that saddens,
Or one that causes pain out of what gladdens.

She married a sweet prince, not one of us.
We should have known our own ordinariness.

The Prince

Before I saw her, I knew what it would be;
Before I knew her, we had a history.
That's how a love is shaped, by its foretelling;
It's like a bell that curves into its pealing.

Before I kissed her, I knew that we would kiss.
Before I touched her, I knew it would be this,
This ache that shapes our courtly narrative,
The way that I was born, so I could live.

And if I tasted on her lips the ambition
I thought would be my kingly right, the momentum
I understood as soon as I gazed into her eyes,
I laughed into the dazzle of surprise.
It would take one of us, and she would do
The climbing for the sun, and for the two.

Snow White

People see me as the good, and as the true,
The reflection of appearance, what they knew
When they were young, and thought the world would happen
As they wished: *Come here, my sweet.* I learned to open

It by learning from the best, and they are
Just human too. Sometimes you kneel awhile
To learn the silver sonnet of a smile,
To rise within the confidence of power.

I grew tired of the queen. She bored me with her tales
Of how she'd governed, velvet in her wiles,
But I would write it down and make a book,
And learn to be a pilgrim and a hook.

I played them all, but that's how people learn.
Come closer. Look into my eyes, and burn.

Part IV

Movies and Literature

"That's how it is on this bitch of an earth."

Pozzo, *Waiting for Godot*

"The stars are ageless."

Norma Desmond, *Sunset Boulevard*

The Hall Is Burning, Barton Fink

The hall is burning, Barton Fink,
And nothing's going quite as planned.
Nothing is quite what you think:

Your self-absorption at the sink.
In theory, life's at your command,
But the hall is burning, Barton Fink.

The shoes, lined up for polish, stink
Of all the things that really happened.
Nothing is quite what you think:

Murder's left its heady ink,
And holding it, you play pretend.
The hall is burning, Barton Fink.

You need some drama, and a shrink.
It's living that makes life profound.
Nothing is quite what you think.

Your prose has no one else to thank.
You've lived your work, too tightly wound.
The hall is burning, Barton Fink.
Nothing is quite what you think.

Norma Desmond Has Some Advice for Betty Schaeffer

Enjoy your body now; of course, you won't.
It's later that you'll stagger with your want
And see the faces turn away from you.
Without their gaze, you won't have much to do.

Don't need the spotlight? Darling, look at me:
Inside this house with Max, Joe, and the monkey.
Think this is what I want? And you are less,
Because you're ordinary, your caress
Just like the touch of others, who are lost—
Pennies to my dollar, found and tossed.

Take my lighter, Sweetheart. Light your way.
Be other than yourself. Be devotee
Of that one face to launch a thousand screens.
Without me, you don't know what romance means.

The Triplets (or Tercets) of Belleville

The three of us make music.
We don't care what we eat.
The outside world is tragic.

We turn away from logic.
We laugh; then we create.
The three of us make music;

The three of us make magic
With broom, and can, and plate.
The outside world is tragic.

We're unapologetic,
And take what we can get.
The three of us make music

As daily anesthetic
For disappointed fate.
The outside world is tragic.

But tripartite aesthetic
Is like laughter, long and sweet.
The three of us make music.
The outside world is tragic.

Vladimir and Estragon Meet with Godot

Act 1.

We find we have some questions. Why the struggle:
The blood, the cross, the yearning? Just for drama?
You didn't *like* us so bereft? Cain, Abel;
The snake, Eve, Adam; oh, who would not dream a
Life that takes the radish, spits it out,
And shapes the dailiness of the devout?

We find you're oddly silent in our hurt.
No, that's not right: more like you've come apart
To dissipate, like rain, or thoughts, in air.
We've always felt you most inside a prayer—

Or most ourselves. Perhaps it's just relief,
This emptiness we can't define. Or loss.
Now that we see you, it is not belief
For Vladimir, and Estragon, and Thomas.

Act 2.

Godot, we're back again; our former awe
Is like the tree and roadside, here and raw.
We're not sure what we are supposed to do.
Clap? Laugh? Be done? Begin again? Now Pozzo
Would consult his watch, and then there's Lucky,
Lost, mad, and chained to self. Somehow, our leaky
Souls always sound a theme, find things to do,
And make a line of footsteps straight to you.

In life, we look for passion, something higher,
To quell our disappointment like a stone.
We kiss a symbol, hurt and love each other,
To fill the gaps between *you* and alone.

Is that your hand? Or is that just a tree?
We thought, once that we met you, we'd be happy.

Nagg and Nell Villanelle

We pop out of a garbage can,
And argue over what is small.
It shows us what we've come to mean—

The thrill that emanates from pain,
The way that we affect at all.
We pop out of a garbage can,

The ash heap and the junk shop scene:
That's where you'll find the older people.
It shows us what we've come to mean.

A gnarly carrot, an old string bean:
There are some who might call this world hell.
We pop out of a garbage can.

We're stuck in love, and we're forgotten:
And so we choose to make life hell.
It shows us what we've come to mean.

We'll take it up a notch, design
A way to make things tolerable.
We pop out of a garbage can.
It shows us what we've come to mean.

Part V

Mythical Women

"No more masks! No more mythologies!
Now, for the first time, the god lifts his hand,
The fragments join in me with their own music."

Muriel Rukeyser, "The Poem as Mask"

The Births of Aphrodite and Athena

The one swirled out of foam, the other mind;
The one disturbs the fish, like bright, lost jacks
Around flung testicles; the other takes
A scholarly approach, as is designed

By scrolls unrolled to myth. The cause of beauty
Is sex; the cause of wisdom is a thought
That shows the hallowed way it must be brought
Into the world. Athena has a duty,

But Aphrodite's an opal of desire,
And though she's born of sea, she makes a fire.
Athena is more cautious, purposeful;
She knows the impulse, yet she acts on rule.
One rises with a kiss, from fields of coral;
The other walks with armor and a moral.

Juliet on Facebook

I saw his Facebook picture, met for chat,
And then the two of us said *that was that,*
Except the world can always change online.
(I knew that already from his Rosaline.)

I felt the Capulets and Montagues
Were always asking the two of us to choose.
And all we wanted was the sweet IM
To jolt us in our bed at 3 AM.

Have you been bullied? That's what it was like:
The dread of all of the comments on the wall,
The feeling that they'll get you, one and all.
When he thought I was dead, it killed his soul.
I had to kill myself, and for his sake.
Now people can make comments: "Like. Dislike."

Ophelia Gives Hamlet a Piece of Her Mind

Hamlet, you thought I was a dirty girl,
And I thought then of what your words could mean.
Now take the fishies of the water's swirl:
They didn't see me dirty, nor as clean,

Just drowned. That's nothing, and that's something too,
Enough to be remembered now by you.
Hamlet, you've always been a narcissist,
But my drowned flowers show you what you've missed:

Someone who's willing to take it all the way.
And if you hesitated at revenge,
Don't think I do. Just watch this water-play,
And how your love grows dear, submerged and strange.

You silked your hand inside my thigh, slept with
My soul. I'm even better as a myth.

Lady Macbeth

"Get the fuck out of my way."

A college administrator explaining
her approach of working with
people, 2008.

There is no compass tilted for the hour
That takes the place of what you feel for power,
The way the world's laid out, like history's toys,
And all you have to do is reach with ease,

And conscience yawning. Some will fuss at fairness—
That quaint old trap—that takes the bite from awareness,
And dulls you to what must be done. Just open
Up your hand. That's how everything must happen.

If blood gets on it, you have to wash it off,
And even in the aftermath of dread
You have to frame your future life instead,
The jewels that ring the furrow of your brow
And all the wills that bend to your knowhow.
Fools will falter, doubt. But you will laugh.

Cordelia Speaks to King Lear of Their Predicament

They decided to destroy us, Father,
And, in the end, there was nothing we could do.
Your neediness held court with all the weather:
They saw the sun, and rain, and moon in you.

I always loved you, your hyperbole;
You loved my candle, plain and ordinary.
To ask me to be different in your yearning
Was to set your kingdom, and your conscience, burning.

Sometimes it takes restraint, not just the show
That fractures all the earth, and sky, with snow.
Father, there are things you do not want to know.
One is that moments change us, even now.
Nights pass. You weep. Blood colors all with dread
And words that never meant the things they said.

The Young and Old of It: Cordelia and Lear Have a Conversation

1.

Oh, Daddy, when you ask for love, you lose
The gift of all that other people choose.
You roar, you walk the echoed halls, you pull
The tablecloth and dishes off the table,

And to what end? To make the others say
What they don't feel, so you can make them pay?
And then, you think, you can make me go one higher,
To prove each older daughter is a liar.

I've had enough of this. My words, gone plain,
Show what the meanings are. Hyperbole
Has no real meaning in a family story.
It is enough for love itself to happen;

It doesn't need to act by other laws.
Love is not made by will, but its own cause.

2.

My darling, you don't know what it can mean
When the others have forgotten you're around,
When what you say becomes what's merely sound.
The old know what a lack of a reaction

Can do. I'm not the first to force the moment,
Not the first to speak the words a little louder,
To get a crowded room to see how torment
Can change the world, and shake the youngest doubter.

I had to turn it up, to get attention,
To get them all. I didn't know how good
The words would feel, not as they really should—
The honey sticking on their daughterhood.

The price, my love lost in a cage, is you.
That is something all my longing can't undo.

Miranda Reviews Her Upbringing, Post-Tempest

1. Five Years Later

I frame my life in "afters" now: the storm,
My years with Caliban, my father's ease
With making all the world take on his eyes.
He saved my life; fed me; and kept me warm:
In short, he was my father, mad with love.

I think I knew I always loved my friend,
My Caliban, my soul. But Ferdinand
Reminded me of Father, in his goals,
A way for me to sugar-coat my roles
Within the world. Some people call that good.

Yet now I know the world as flat, bereft.
Our sameness, strangely, sets us both adrift.
There's something missing, the essential of
Myself. Sometimes we mistake *love* for *should.*

2. Ten Years Later

You do not get them back, you know: the days
You thought were perfect. Yet somehow you knew
That you had spent them with a squandered ease.
Sometimes at night I think of him, the flow

Of devotion, how in all the world, we found
Each other, a coincidence profound
As any religion prayed for in the world.
I know that now.

                    Meanwhile, the pennant's unfurled
With majesty. I yawn. I think of him:
The way we found our unshaped lives together,
How, there between us, we were son and daughter.
Prospero was flawed, but awed, we held the hem
Of magic. Through Father, the two of us would join,
And either way we landed, the same coin.

3. At the End of Her Life

My father knew the world could shrink to the size
Of an instrument, a way to map and know
What was unknown. Life's like that too: the brew
Of daily life reduced, at last, to cries

Of pain and pleasure, best and worst, the epic—
Or what we see as epic—of our lives.
I don't know who I was, kaleidoscopic,
Like leaves before they hit the ground as leaves,

Or like the fragrant billowing of sleeves
On a day when after-talk is done on pillows,
And dressing seems arcane. Funny how this grieves
Me most, to think of this. We take what follows,

But always there's a choice. A word. A vow.
Whatever happens, we live on somehow.

Penelope Sets the Record Straight

They mistranslated "text" and thought the "weave"
Was a material, through which I'd grieve
And keep my suitors at the door, undoing
A day's work. Naturally, I liked to keep them going,
Keep them patient, while I waited for Ulysses.

But text is writing; text is a catharsis.
And I'm clairvoyant with a spouse's mourning,

Please know in twenty years something is burning:

Not just the towers, smoke in every heart,
But all the bitterness of time apart.
The journey that's interior has weight,
Outside the ship and all affairs of state.
I'm writing and rewriting: not done quite.
To say something, you have to say it right.

Leda

I'm tired of all the games: the giant swan,
The other transformations you tried on.
With every thought equated to an action,
You didn't blame yourself. Just liked the sheen
Of fear tied up in rope, and stiff with blood.
You liked the way you shamed and sullied good.

But listen to me now: I'm done. I'm human,
Sick of all the things gods do to women,
Your narcissism clear, your shifting weathers,
The sudden suffocation by your feathers.

I'm cleaning myself off, to find a moral.
See yourself for what you are: a debacle
On a cloud. On earth, we find it different, Zeus.
Look: all the ropes you tied me with are loose.

On Bullying

*Adults need to be more proactive in all cases, but particularly in cases that involve young people.

*People expect that victims are not high achieving or well liked, but often the opposite is true. Envy can be the source of the problem.

*People tend to look the other way when mobbing or bullying is taking place. When organizations protect themselves over the individual, it can be dispiriting to others, and ultimately hurt, or destroy, the organization.

*People who speak out—who observe mobbing and bullying—can change the course of history. In the end, the powerlessness of not reporting the behavior can be detrimental to witnesses, as well as the victims of the bullying.

*Bullying can result in suicide, and suicide is the single greatest cause of death for people under the age of 14.

Resources on Bullying

Davenport, Noa, Ruth D. Schwartz, and Gail Pursell Elliott.
Mobbing: Emotional Abuse in the American Workplace.
Ames: Civil Society Pub., 1999.

Twale, Darla S., and Barbara DeLuca. *Faculty Incivility: The
Rise of the Academic Bully Culture and What to Do About
it.* San Francisco: Jossey-Bass, 2008.

Westhues, Kenneth. *The Envy of Excellence: Administrative
Mobbing of High-Achieving Professors.* Lewiston: Edwin
Mellen Press, 2005.

www.bullyonline/schoolbully/cases.htm

www.pacer.org/bullying/resources

www.stopbullying.gov

www.workplacebullying.org

Acknowledgments

This book was supported by a CASSDA grant at West Chester, which gave me the time and peace to finish this book.

I also continue to be grateful to Dana Gioia, who has made this transition as smooth as it could be.

Acumen: "Persephone Falls in Love with Hades," "Persephone Finds Many Aspects of Her Life Have Changed," "Persephone Leads a Double Life"

American Arts Quarterly: From "The Desdemona Sonnets": "The Pillow to the Handkerchief"

Barrow Street: From "The Desdemona Sonnets": "Desdemona to Othello," "Othello to Desdemona"

Cimarron Review: "Watching"

Connecticut Review: "Before Jumping Off the Bridge," "Mobbing," "Song in the Canoe"

First Things: "The Births of Aphrodite and Athena," "Juliet on Facebook"

The Georgia Review: "Genealogy"

Innisfree Poetry Journal: "Vladimir and Estragon Meet with Godot"

Poem: From "The Desdemona Sonnets":"Iago to the Audience"

Tilt-a-Whirl: "Somewhere" "The Triplets (or Tercets) of Belleville"

Tower Journal: "Blood Doesn't Have Your Name," "Cordelia Speaks to King Lear of Their Predicament," "Evil," "Flowers," "The Hall Is Burning, Barton Fink," "Leda," "Norma Desmond Has Some Advice for Betty Schaeffer," "Paradise," "Penelope Sets the Record Straight," "Ruined People," "Sit"

Umbrella: "Brokenness"

About the Author

Kim Bridgford is the director of the West Chester University Poetry Center and the West Chester University Poetry Conference, the largest all-poetry writing conference in the United States. As editor of *Mezzo Cammin,* she was the founder of The *Mezzo Cammin* Women Poets Timeline Project, which was launched at the National Museum of Women in the Arts in Washington on March 27, 2010, and will eventually be the largest database of women poets in the world. She is the author of seven books of poetry: *Undone* (David Robert Books); *Instead of Maps* (David Robert Books); *In the Extreme: Sonnets about World Records* (Story Line Press), winner of the Donald Justice Prize; *Take-Out: Sonnets about Fortune Cookies* (David Robert Books); *Hitchcock's Coffin: Sonnets about Classic Films* (David Robert Books); *Bully Pulpit* (White Violet Press); and the forthcoming *Epiphanies* (David Robert Books, 2013), Her work has been nominated for the Pulitzer Prize, the Poets' Prize, and six times for a Pushcart Prize.

During her tenure at Fairfield University, she became known as one of the best writing program directors in the United States, a teacher of national reputation (a former Connecticut Professor of the Year and two-time nominee for U.S. Professor of the Year), and one of the best contemporary practitioners of the sonnet. She was the 2007 Connecticut Touring Poet, a series that has included Robert Pinsky, X. J. Kennedy, James Merrill, and Donald Justice.

Her collaborative work with visual artist Jo Yarrington on Iceland, Venezuela, and Bhutan has been honored by a Ucross residency, and has appeared in exhibitions, at conferences, and in journals such as *The Iowa Review, Connecticut Review, The Lyric,* and *The Robert Frost Review.*

Her collaborative work with the Printmakers' Network of Southern New England and poets Sue Standing and Vivian Shipley—the three-book set entitled *Travel*—has been featured at Fairfield University, Wheaton College, the University of Connecticut, and many other venues.

Bridgford has received grants from the National Endowment for the Arts and the Connecticut Commission on the Arts. Her work has appeared on *The Writer's Almanac* with Garrison Keillor, four times on *Verse Daily*, and has been honored by the Catholic Press Association of the United States and Canada. She has appeared in *The New York Times, The Washington Post, The Philadelphia Inquirer, The Chronicle of Higher Education,* and *The Connecticut Post;* on NPR and the website of *The News Hour with Jim Lehrer;* and in various headline news outlets.

She wrote the introduction to Russell Goings' *The Children of Children Keep Coming*, an epic griot song, and joined Goings in ringing the closing bell of the New York Stock Exchange when the book was released, a week before the Obama inauguration.

www.ingramcontent.com/pod-product-compliance
Lightning Source LLC
LaVergne TN
LVHW021612080426
835510LV00019B/2538